Got a License But Where Do I go?

Devotions for Teens on the Move

Got a License But Where Do I

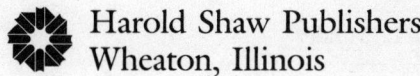

Harold Shaw Publishers
Wheaton, Illinois

DALE and SANDY LARSEN

Got a License, But Where Do I Go?

Copyright © 1988 by Dale and Sandy Larsen

All rights reserved.
No part of this book
may be reproduced or transmitted
in any form or by any means,
electronic or mechanical,
including photocopying, recording,
or any information storage and retrieval system
without written permission
from Harold Shaw Publishers,
Box 567, Wheaton, Illinois 60189.

ISBN 0-87788-333-5

Cover and interior design: K. L. Mulder

Cover photo: Jim Whitmer

Library of Congress Cataloging-in-Publication Data

Larsen, Dale.
   Got a license, but where do I go? : devotions for teens on the move / Dale and Sandy Larsen.
      p. cm.
   Summary: A collection of devotional readings for teens concerning decision making, ethics, and mature behavior.
   ISBN 0-87788-295-9
   1. Youth—Prayer-books and devotions—English. [1. Prayer books and devotions. 2. Conduct of life. 3. Christian life.]
I. Larsen, Sandy. II. Title.
BV4531.2.L34 1988
248.8'3—dc19   87-36576
                                                                CIP
                                                                 AC

97 96 95 94 93 92 91 90 89 88

10 9 8 7 6 5 4 3 2 1

☐ CONTENTS

Week One: But I Hate to Make Decisions...

1. Just a Nibble Won't Hurt *Genesis 3:6* — 3
2. Looks Aren't Everything *Genesis 13:9-12* — 5
3. Have I Gotta Plan for God! *Genesis 16:1-2, 5* — 7
4. Hasty Words—Lengthy Regrets *Matthew 14:6-9* — 9
5. A Chance to Come Back *Luke 15:11-24* — 13

Week Two: The Source of Right and the Reason for Wrong

1. God Is Great—God Is Good! *Exodus 20:1-17* — 19
2. It's Up to Me? *Deuteronomy 30:15-20* — 23
3. Problem People *Isaiah 58:6-14* — 25
4. Judgment Joy! *Psalm 96* — 27
5. The Judge Who Served the Sentence *1 Timothy 1:15-17* — 29

Week Three: The Giver of Choices

1. If You Want a Peach Tree... *Luke 6:43-45* — 33
2. Treasures and Choices *Matthew 6:19-21* — 35
3. Deeper than Skin Deep *1 Samuel 16:6-13* — 37
4. Who Can I Trust? *Matthew 6:25-34* — 39
5. Heart Makeover *Jeremiah 31:31-34* — 41

Week Four: Forks in the Road

1. Easy to Say, Hard to Do *John 13:34-35* — 45
2. Jesus' Top Two *Mark 12:28-31* — 47
3. Fatal Envy *1 John 3:11-12* — 49
4. Love in Action *1 John 3:16-18* — 51
5. The Source of My Choices *1 John 4:7-12* — 53

Week Five: What's Easy and What's Right

1. Something to Stand On   *Psalm 19:7-11* — 57
2. Okay for Me, Tough for You   *Matthew 18:21-35* — 59
3. Hold on... He's Holding onto You
   Psalm 119:33-40 — 61
4. When Trouble Knocks, Don't Answer
   Proverbs 1:10-19 — 63
5. Now and Forever   *Psalm 119:89-91* — 65

Week Six: My Choices and My Friends

1. Bickering Is for Babies   *1 Corinthians 3:1-5* — 69
2. Attitude Check   *Romans 14:1-4* — 71
3. Different Worship for Different People
   Romans 14:5-7 — 73
4. Yeah, but He's Wrong!   *Galatians 6:1-2* — 75
5. For My Friend's Sake   *Romans 14:19-21* — 79

Week Seven: The High Cost of Jesus' Choice

1. He Gave Up Heaven   *Philippians 2:5-8* — 83
2. Just Say No—to Yourself!   *Luke 9:23-25* — 85
3. Finishing What You Start   *Luke 14:28-30* — 87
4. Last Place?   *Mark 9:33-35* — 89
5. The Shepherd Pays   *John 10:11-15* — 91

Week Eight: Real-life Choices: What Would Jesus Choose?

1. When Temptation Bugs You...   *Hebrews 5:7-9* — 95
2. Slammed Doors, Blocked Plans   *Acts 16:6-10* — 97
3. Thanks or No Thanks?   *Luke 17:11-19* — 99
4. He Could Have Passed By   *Luke 10:30-35* — 101
5. Jesus Chose His Father's Way   *Matthew 26:39-46* — 103

☐ Week・One

But I *Hate* to Make Decisions . . .

☐ DAY ONE

Just a Nibble Won't Hurt

"*B*oy, if *I'd* been in the garden of Eden, I wouldn't have blown human history by eating a dumb apple!"

You've read the story from Genesis 3 before.

> *When the woman saw that the fruit of the tree was good for food and pleasing to the eye, and also desirable for gaining wisdom, she took some and ate it. She also gave some to her husband, who was with her, and he ate it.* Genesis 3:6

Well, why not? The fruit looked good, she imagined it would taste good, and it promised a new kind of knowledge—the knowledge of what it would be like to disobey God for the first time.

A Decision ... a Disaster!

So Eve took the innocent-looking fruit, and WHAM!—humanity took its long tumble down the miserable path of sin. Envy, killing, idolatry, rape, and war followed in short order. Far down the road God would have to pay the ultimate price of his Son before humankind would be restored to God; and even then, things would never again be what they were in Eden.

What a stupid thing for Eve to do, right?

But wait a minute. Was Eve's decision that different from the "little" decisions you make every day? Do you ever crave something that's not yours, for example? Or congratulate yourself for "getting away with something"? Do you ever deliberately plan to disobey God when you know better?

Choices Have Consequences

Okay, we don't have the fate of mankind hanging in the balance like Adam and Eve did. But when we make our decisions, we do have the welfare of our own souls and bodies hanging in the balance—not to mention the welfare of all the people around us who are affected by how we live.

Say you choose to give a classmate an unkind nickname like "Geek" or "Bozo" or worse—or to perpetuate one that others gave him. Your words wound that person's spirit. If he hears the cruel names often enough from people whose opinions count with him, they rob the joy from his teenage years. Can you think of a person in your school or church who you've wounded with unkind words? When you decide to give that person encouraging words, you can make his life worth living!

Your Decisions Count

Everything we decide to do changes us a little bit—or a lot. It also changes the lives of other people. We're constantly shaping the world within us and the world around us.

Today, as you pray, you might want to say something to God along these lines:

"Lord, I need your help. What I decide to do today will make a difference in my life and other people's lives, now and forever. I'm not even aware of all the decisions I make. Show me where I'm making good decisions, and where my decisions need to come under your direction. Help me as I have to decide about _____ . And thanks, Lord, for being here to guide me in my decisions, because I'm not wise enough to know what to do."

☐ DAY TWO

Looks Aren't Everything

Wouldn't it be nice to have a weekend job that gave you lots of spending money, even if it meant you had to work with people who weren't the best influence? Or wouldn't it be great to get into the most exclusive club in school, even if its members are known for doing some things you know you shouldn't? Or wouldn't it feel good to win all the school extra-curricular awards, even if it kept you so busy you didn't have much time for your family?

Range War

Abraham's nephew Lot found out that the glitter of easy living disguises danger and loss.

The dust cloud could be seen for miles around when Abraham was on the move. His giant herds of sheep and cattle looked like something out of an "eastern Western." Lot, traveling with his uncle, had his own flocks and herds, and soon there was competition for grazing land.

Abraham wanted to keep the peace. He said to Lot:

> "Is not the whole land before you? Let's part company. If you go to the left, I'll go to the right; if you go to the right, I'll go to the left."

> *Lot looked up and saw that the whole plain of the Jordan was well watered . . . So Lot chose for himself the whole plain of the Jordan and set out toward the east . . . Lot lived among the cities of the plain and pitched his tents near Sodom.*
> Genesis 13:9-12

Good Land, Bad Company

Great, right? Except that when Lot chose the best land, he chose the worst company. "Now the men of Sodom were wicked and were sinning greatly against the Lord" (13:13). That was an understatement! The New Testament says that in Sodom Lot was "distressed by the filthy lives of lawless men (for that righteous man, living among them day after day, was tormented in his righteous soul by the lawless deeds he saw and heard)" (2 Peter 2:7-8).

Lot was upset by Sodom, but not upset enough to leave. He didn't want to offend the people, and besides, he was making money there. For a while his prosperity outweighed his conscience. When God finally judged and destroyed the place, two angels literally had to drag Lot out of town at the last minute, and he lost everything.

Choose Carefully

Where did Lot get himself into trouble? Write down the decision that brought him trouble instead of paradise.

_____

_____

Lot chose what looked good, without thinking about what he might be getting himself into morally.

What pulls you with the promise of ease and comfort? Pray about your desires, along these lines: "Lord, I want _____

_____very much, but I'm not sure if it's good for me. What do *you* want for me? Keep me from pursuing what isn't best for me, no matter how attractive it looks. I especially need your

help with my desire for _____ . Thank you for guarding my spirit and for caring about what's best for me."

WEEK ONE

☐ DAY THREE

Have I Gotta Plan for God!

Ever get impatient with God for not doing what he's "supposed" to, at the time you think he should? Then you can sympathize with Abraham and Sarah (whose names were still Abram and Sarai at this point). God had promised them a son, and when the promise took more years than they thought it should, they decided to help God along.

> Now Sarai, Abram's wife, had borne him no children. But she had an Egyptian maidservant named Hagar; so she said to Abram, ". . . Go, sleep with my maidservant; perhaps I can build a family through her." Abram agreed to what Sarai said. Genesis 16:1-2

A Success—Sort of

The scheme sounded like an ideal solution. And it "worked"—Hagar did become pregnant. But the threesome hadn't counted on the emotions involved. Hagar lorded it over Sarai, and Sarai was jealous.

> Then Sarai said to Abram, "You are responsible for the wrong I am suffering. I put my servant in your arms, and now that she knows she is pregnant, she despises me. May the Lord judge between you and me." Genesis 16:5

Did God Ask for Help?

Sometimes we get as impatient as Abraham and Sarah. Maybe you're sixteen and have never had a date, or you haven't met that Right Person yet. Or maybe God hasn't changed your misunderstanding parents. Or he hasn't given you a full understanding of trigonometry, or the backhand to be the top-seeded tennis player. What are some things you get anxious about and want to take over instead of leaving them in God's hands?

_____

_____

_____

The World Is Still Paying

So we "help" God along like Abraham and Sarah helped him along. Their sad story didn't end with a few hard feelings between Sarah and Hagar. Sarah drove Hagar away, but she came back and had a son, Ishmael. Abraham and Sarah finally had the son God had *really* promised (Isaac). Then there was rivalry between Isaac and Ishmael, and Sarah drove off Hagar and Ishmael for good.

Isaac's descendants are the Jews, and Ishmael's descendants are the Arabs. They have never gotten over their rivalry. Sarah and Abraham's "assistance" for the Lord has made the world sorry ever since.

Our decisions have consequences that stretch into future generations. When we let God do things his way, our decisions will make the future happier, not sadder.

Pray about Impatience

Check out your list of areas where you'd like God to do things faster or more to your liking. Hard as it is, surrender those things to him as you talk to him in prayer now. You could pray something like, "Lord, I'm impatient about _____. I know you're God, and I want to let you be God in this area of my life too. Help me wait—and even to give up this wish if you want me to. I'd still rather have your will than anything."

W·E·E·K O·N·E

☐ DAY FOUR

Hasty Words—Lengthy Regrets

"If only I hadn't said . . ."

What was the last thing you said that you feel sorry for now? "I hate you!" "Sure, I'll do anything for you!" "I never want to see you again!"

Hasty words tend to backfire on us. "Be quick to listen, slow to speak" says James 1:19, and King Herod is a terrific demonstration of why that good advice is in the Bible.

Herod had stolen his brother's wife, Herodias, even though (1) he was already married, and (2) she was his niece, the daughter of another brother of his. John the Baptist, never known for saying what was easy and popular, told him the arrangement was all wrong. Herod put John in prison, but let him live because he was afraid to destroy such a righteous man.

A Dangerous Dinner

Herodias didn't share Herod's fears; she hated John and wanted to get rid of him forever. Her fatal opportunity came at Herod's birthday party.

> On Herod's birthday the daughter of Herodias danced for them and pleased Herod so much that he promised with an oath to give her whatever she asked. Prompted by her mother,

she said, "Give me here on a platter the head of John the Baptist." The king was distressed, but because of his oaths and his dinner guests, he ordered that her request be granted.
Matthew 14:6-9

John lost his life over Herod's hasty words.

The king's first, impulsive decision—telling the girl she could have anything she asked for—was foolish enough. It sprang from boastfulness, lust, and probably too much to drink. His worse decision was the one he thought about more carefully: he weighed John's life against "his oaths and his dinner guests" and decided John's life was less valuable.

Fatal Pride

Making a bad decision isn't always the end of the road. God is merciful, and he often gives us an opportunity to think twice and change our minds. Usually people will understand if we swallow our pride and are courageous enough to say, "I was wrong. I spoke too soon. I'm sorry."

Herod didn't swallow his pride. He let it choke him into doing something he regretted. His guests had heard his boastful vow, and he didn't want to look foolish in front of them. So Herod saved face, and John lost his head.

Herod regretted his action as long as he lived. As soon as he heard about Jesus, Herod said, "This is John the Baptist; he has risen from the dead!" (Matthew 14:2). John was very much on Herod's guilty mind.

A Second Chance

God may be providing you with an opportunity to change a hasty decision. Think over the last few weeks. Are there words or choices you wish you could take back?

_____

_____

Ask him to show you if he has ways to undo a poor choice you've made.

Pray also that you'll stop and think before you choose too quickly—whether it's what to say to your parents this morning, whether to skip classes today, where to go tonight, or any other choices that come up. Ask the Lord, rather than your impulses, to guide you. And he will!

☐ DAY FIVE

A Chance to Come Back

So you blew it! You made a wrong decision and you're paying the consequences. The car you bought spends more time in the shop than on the road. You went out for the golf team instead of orchestra, and now the orchestra is going to Europe. The person you broke up with too quickly is dating somebody else now and has no interest in getting back together with you.

Maybe you deeply regret a far more serious choice. You were showing off and you injured yourself in some way that will never be healed. Or you gave away your sexual purity in a moment of "Who cares?" Those things happen—yes, even to Christians.

Now What?

So what do you do now? Hate yourself for the rest of your life? That's not very constructive!

God has a better idea: repentance. He offers us a chance to start over. He doesn't promise to *undo* all the results of our bad decisions, but he does offer to forgive us and take us back to himself. Then, equipped with his Spirit, we can go on and make something better out of the future.

Repentance, and the Father's welcoming love, is the point of Jesus' best-known and best-loved parable, the "prodigal son" (Luke 15:11-31).

A String of Bad Choices

If anybody ever made wrong choices, it was the younger son in this parable.

> *"There was a man who had two sons. The younger one said to his father, 'Father, give me my share of the estate.' So he divided his property between them.*
>
> *"Not long after that, the younger son got together all he had, set off for a distant country and there squandered his wealth in wild living. After he had spent everything, there was a severe famine in that whole country, and he began to be in need. So he went and hired himself out to a citizen of that country, who sent him to his fields to feed pigs. He longed to fill his stomach with the pods that the pigs were eating, but no one gave him anything."* Luke 15:11-16

That could have been the end of the story—a good object lesson in the results of bad choices. But Jesus was not illustrating bad choices; he was illustrating God's love.

> *"When he came to his senses, he said, 'How many of my father's hired men have food to spare, and here I am starving to death! I will set out and go back to my father and say to him: Father, I have sinned against heaven and against you. I am no longer worthy to be called your son; make me like one of your hired men.' So he got up and went to his father.*
>
> *"But while he was still a long way off, his father saw him and was filled with compassion for him; he ran to his son, threw his arms around him and kissed him.*
>
> *"The son said to him, 'Father I have sinned against heaven and against you, I am no longer worthy to be called your son.'*
>
> *"But the father said to his servants, 'Quick! Bring the best robe and put it on him. Put a ring on his finger and sandals on his feet. Bring the fattened calf and kill it. Let's have a feast and celebrate. For this son of mine was dead and is alive again; he was lost and is found.'"* Luke 15:17-24

The son asked only to be treated as a hired servant. His father took him back as a son, complete with gifts and celebrations! That's what God does for us when we come to him through Christ.

Making All Things New

Repenting doesn't turn back the clock. It won't restore what we threw away in our foolishness. It *does* bring us into relationship with Jesus, who makes "all things new" (Revelation 21:5, KJV).

Have you made choices that still haunt you? Talk with God about them specifically now. Maybe you're punishing yourself for them but have never repented and accepted God's mercy. Jesus died for that foolish choice; accept his forgiveness by saying,

"Lord, thank you for dying for _____.
Thank you that I'm clean in your sight now because you paid the

cost for me. Give me a clean start in the areas of _____

_____."

☐ *Week · Two*

The Source of *Right* and the Reason for *Wrong*

W·E·E·K T·W·O

☐ DAY ONE
God Is Great— God Is Good!

Imagine a world where people . . .
  put God first
  don't have phony "gods" like money and power, but instead honor the one true God
  say the Lord's name with respect and not as an all-purpose swear word
  spend the Lord's day peacefully by worshiping him and resting, not in frantic activity which leaves him out
  honor their parents even if the parents aren't perfect
  respect life and don't kill, either in action or attitude
  respect marriage and stay faithful to their partners
  respect each other's property and don't take what isn't theirs
  tell the truth about each other and don't falsely accuse each other
  are happy with what they have and don't get bitter about what other people have.

A Good Place to Live

What would it be like to live in a world like that? You can fill in the details:
  In a world like that, I wouldn't have to worry about:

I wouldn't have to be afraid other people would:

___

My relationships would be:

___

The Good Commandments

That's the kind of life people would have if everyone lived by the Ten Commandments.

> *And God spoke all these words:*
> *"You shall have no other gods before me.*
> *"You shall not make for yourself an idol in the form of anything in heaven above or in the waters below. . . .*
> *"You shall not misuse the name of the Lord your God . . ."*
> *"Remember the Sabbath day by keeping it holy. . . .*
> *"Honor your father and mother . . .*
> *"You shall not murder.*
> *"You shall not commit adultery.*
> *"You shall not steal.*
> *"You shall not give false testimony against your neighbor.*
> *"You shall not covet your neighbor's house . . . wife . . . manservant or maidservant, his ox or donkey, or anything that belongs to your neighbor."* Exodus 20:1-17

Though some people mistakenly think the Ten Commandments are a set of narrow, out-dated, stifling rules, it's easy to see that God gave us the commandments for our own good. Obeying them is in our best interests.

How did God dream up these great commandments? He didn't pick them out of a hat. They come from his character. They are good because *he* is good. They're about things which are vital to him: life, love, and the truth that only he is God.

Thanks for Caring

As you pray, thank the Lord for caring enough about you and the whole rest of the human race to give you good rules for your happiness. If you have trouble finding your own words of thanks, here are some ideas: "Lord, thank you for caring about us—and about me. I see now that you've made your rules because you love us and don't want us to hurt ourselves and each other. I'm especially glad for your law about _____.

The one that's hardest for me is your law about _____; help me obey you. I'm glad my life is in your hands because you're a good and great God!"

W·E·E·K T·W·O

☐ DAY TWO

It's Up to Me?

"I'd like to be given a little more responsibility around here! Doesn't anybody think I'm competent?"

Ever heard that complaint on the yearbook staff or the homecoming committee or the church youth group? Maybe you've made it yourself.

Your Choices Matter

Everybody wants to be thought of as mature and responsible. Okay—what if you were responsible for choosing the outcome of your life? What if God considered you so responsible that he let you choose the direction of your life—now and after you die?

"Wait a minute! I want to be responsible, but not THAT responsible!"

Well, before you run the other direction, stop and read Deuteronomy 30:15-20. God said these things to the Israelites just before they went into the land he'd promised them.

> *I have set before you life and death, blessings and curses. Now choose life, so that you and your children may live and that you may love the Lord your God, listen to his voice, and hold fast to him. For the Lord is your life* . . . Deuteronomy 30:19-20

People, Not Computers

God was only being fair to the people. He was telling them that the way to live happily in the new land was to continue to follow him, and the way to be miserable was to reject him. He presented the people with their alternatives.

God created human beings with free choice. He could have programmed us to "love" him and "obey" him, but that wouldn't have been real love and obedience. Nobody can force you to love or obey anybody else; it has to come from your heart, freely decided by you.

The Choice Is Up to Us

So what does God have on this earth? A few billion free-spirited people who need to obey him for their own good. What does he do with us? He tells us what we should do, but he leaves the choice up to us.

Scary, huh? But also a tremendous gift from the Creator and a huge act of respect for his creations. God lets you choose whether to love him or not.

That choice isn't a one-time thing—it's every day. Make your choice for him now as you pray: "Lord, I'm choosing you today. When other things pull me away from you, remind me that you come first. Specifically, I want your way in _____. Thank you for trusting me with this choice, and help me always to honor you by my choices."

☐ DAY THREE

Problem People

I'm feeling good about the Lord today. I really want to serve him. Now here comes Nasty Foulmouth down the hall at school. There's no escape. He goes for me like a magnet. I don't know if he'll trip me, lie about me, or beg to borrow my math homework, but he's sure to do something I can't stand.

I silently beg God to get Nasty out of my life, but I have a nagging feeling that God has put Nasty there for a reason. Why? So I can decide whether I actually mean what I say about following God. If I love God, I'll find some way to love Nasty Foulmouth too, even if it kills me.

God's Priorities

God's standard of right and wrong is much more personal than "Go to church" and "Avoid the bad crowd." The choices he puts in front of us every day are often choices about how we're going to act, think, and speak toward another human being—usually a human being who rubs us the wrong way.

At one point the Hebrew people thought they had done all the "religious" things God requires, including fasting, and still he wasn't blessing them. But they were missing the point of what God really wanted. Through the prophet Isaiah, God told them:

> *If you do away with the yoke of oppression, with the pointing finger and malicious talk, and if you spend yourselves in behalf of the hungry and satisfy the needs of the oppressed, then your light will rise in the darkness, and your night will become like the noonday.* Isaiah 58:9b-10

Read Isaiah 58:6-14 to get more of how much the Lord values our treatment of each other. (While you're at it, why not read the entire chapter?)

People First

As good as religious activity is, it's no substitute for really loving other people. It's easier to go to church, choir practice, and youth group than it is to love a difficult person. Don't stop going to church, but *do* decide to care about people who need love.

Pray for people you don't get along with or who bother you. Specific people, not just "everybody who's difficult"! Make a short list here.

_____

_____

Pray along these lines: "Lord, with your help, I'm making the conscious decision to love _____ no matter what. But you're going to have to help me, because I don't have that kind of unselfish love in me. Thank you for living in me and loving through me. I need you every minute today!"

☐ DAY FOUR

Judgment Joy!

> Let the heavens rejoice, let the earth be glad;
> let the sea resound, and all that is in it;
> let the fields be jubilant, and everything in them.
> Then all the trees of the forest will sing for joy;
> they will sing before the Lord, for he comes,
> he comes to judge the earth.
> He will judge the world in righteousness
> and the peoples in his truth. Psalm 96:11-13

We usually think of the judgment of God as something to tremble in fear about. But the psalm you just read makes it the object of a song of joy and praise. Even the trees, fields, and oceans, it says, are going to be glad about God's judgment!

What's There to Be Glad about?

What's going on here? Why all this joy? Because this coming Judge is *fair*. I think of how often I yell, "That's not fair!" when life deals me a low blow or a bad hand. Isn't it good to know that when God decides something, it's right, and when he says something, it's true!

No fooling, lies, or dishonesty with *this* Judge! And needless to say, no bribes either!

So What?

What difference does it make to know God is fair? Just this: it means I know his laws are right. If he puts restrictions on me (which he does), it's not because he's a cranky fun-spoiler, but because he wants what's best for me and for everybody.

For example, he puts curbs on my selfish desires so I won't hurt anybody else. He restricts other people so they won't hurt me. It all works together to make harmony—*when* we obey him.

When I want to rebel and go against God's laws, it helps to remember that his laws are fair and right. I'll only be tangling myself up in grief if I go against him.

List three of God's rules that seem to restrict but actually protect you and others.

_____

_____

_____

Be Glad God Is God

In prayer we have the privilege of talking to One who is fair and who loves us. A good idea for your prayers today would be to read Psalm 96 again and "spring" your own prayers off it. Like this [verse 4]: "For great is the Lord and most worthy of praise; he is to be feared above all gods. Thank you, Lord, that you're bigger than any false god. I know I'm tempted to worship the

false god of _____ but I want to worship you instead—joyfully! You deserve all my praise. Today I'll especially

honor you by _____ . I praise you for being right and fair even when I'm not and other people aren't. You're the One I can count on!"

☐ DAY FIVE

The Judge Who Served the Sentence

So the God who makes the rules for me is fair, right, and true. Is that much comfort when I've broken his laws? Sure he'll judge me fairly—but he'll *still* judge me, right? There's good news for everybody who has broken God's laws. He is not only our Judge; he is our Savior.

Who's the Worst?

Nobody appreciated God's mercy more than Paul did. He considered himself very "religious" when he denied Christ and persecuted Christians. When the Lord stopped him cold and showed him that Jesus was real, Paul made the wise decision to give up his self-righteousness and accept Christ's righteousness. Later he wrote this:

> Here is a trustworthy saying that deserves full acceptance: Christ Jesus came into the world to save sinners—of whom I am the worst. But for that very reason I was shown mercy so that in me, the worst of sinners, Christ Jesus might display his unlimited patience as an example for those who would believe on him and receive eternal life. Now to the King eternal, immortal, invisible, the only God, be honor and glory for ever and ever. Amen. 1 Timothy 1:15-17

"Paul's the worst sinner?" you ask. "Oh yeah? He doesn't know my buddy down the street—or even me at times!"

Well, regardless of who's the champion sinner, Christ died for all of us to make God's forgiveness available to us. God's amazing news is that our Judge has also stepped down to serve our sentence for us. He freely provides the way out for everyone who has disobeyed him—if only we turn back to him and accept his mercy.

Honoring Him

Seeing God the Judge as Savior too didn't make God wishy-washy in Paul's eyes. Verse 17 is one of the most worshipful sentences you'll find in the Bible. Say it to the Lord now as the beginning of your prayers. Add your own praises as you think about how he saved you! You can honor him for

- his love for you
- his patience with you
- his willingness to sacrifice himself
- his eternal life which he shares with you
- something special which he's done for you recently
- anything else you want to praise him for today.

Week · Three

The Giver of Choices

☐ DAY ONE

If You Want a Peach Tree...

If you want a peach tree... you plant a peach pit, of course. You don't plant a zucchini seed or an apple seed or a banana... (what do you plant for bananas?)

I once planted several packages of seeds a friend had given me. They were old seeds and I doubted if they would come up. I was delighted when one of the rows soon flourished with green bean seedlings. As I tended the rest of the garden that summer, the green beans appeared to be taking good care of themselves. They soon had blossoms, then pods...

Wait a minute. These didn't look like green bean pods. They were something mysterious. Where was that package? I'd thrown it out. All I could do was wait and see what the mystery plants produced. In a few weeks they were obviously Chinese edible-pod beans. Nope—the pods were tough and chewy. Aw, come on, what *are* these things?

What You Plant, Grows

Finally I broke open a swelling pod to find three familiar light-green disks inside. Taste settled the question once and for all. *Lima beans*! I could not remember planting lima beans, but there they were. Even if the package had been labelled wrong, there was absolutely no doubt that what I had planted was lima beans because lima beans were what came up.

Jesus used the same gardening principle to illustrate the fact that how we *live* grows from who we *are, inside:*

> *No good tree bears bad fruit, nor does a bad tree bear good fruit. Each tree is recognized by its own fruit. People do not pick figs from thornbushes, or grapes from briers. The good man brings good things out of the good stored up in his heart, and the evil man brings evil things out of the evil stored up in his heart. For out of the overflow of his heart his mouth speaks.*
> Luke 6:43-45

Growing from the Inside Out

Are you displeased with the decisions you make? Maybe you keep saying "prickly" things because there's a thornbush in your heart. Maybe you act disrespectful to your teachers because, inside, you *don't* respect them. Make a short list of some of the decisions you've made that you're not so happy about.

_____

_____

Instead of trying to fix up your behavior, let God renew you from the inside out.

All the good things we call the "fruit of the Spirit"—love, joy, peace, patience, kindness, goodness, faithfulness, gentleness, and self-control (Galatians 5:22-23)—can only be grown by the Holy Spirit within us. When we're short on those qualities, we need to give him more of our inner selves.

Praying from the Inside Out

Before this day gets any further along, let God examine your heart to see what you're growing there. Think of particular areas like home life, school, friends, work, sports, or the opposite sex. Don't be afraid to be specific, as in "Lord, I'm feeding my hateful attitude toward _____ and I'm jealous of _____ . Replace my wrong attitudes with your love so the fruit I bear will be the best fruit possible for you."

☐ DAY TWO

Treasures and Choices

In the bedroom wall of a house we used to live in there was a mysterious locked compartment. After we tried to get it open and couldn't, we speculated often about what was in it. Stocks and bonds? Gold coins? A deed? A will? A lock of long blond hair tied with a ribbon? The clue to a murder?

Finally we located a key and got the strange little door open. Inside was an ugly lamp and a lot of dust.

Everybody Has Treasure

Some treasure! But obviously the lamp was important enough to somebody, sometime, to lock away—though not important enough to take along when they moved out.

One person's treasure is another person's junk. The truth is, everybody has treasure, and what we "treasure" affects all the choices we make.

What do you value more than anything in the world? It may not be a material thing; it might be other people's praise. Or it may be money, your own physical skills, another person, even a record collection and the status it brings. To you, it's gold. What is that most valuable thing?

What's in Your Wall Safe?

Jesus said that when we value anything, something funny happens to our hearts. Our hearts follow right along after what we value. And that affects how we live.

For example, if you put ultimate value on your favorite Wednesday-night TV show, you'll never be happy sitting in youth group on Wednesday nights; your heart will keep tugging you back to the TV set. Here's how Christ put it:

> *Do not store up for yourselves treasures on earth, where moth and rust destroy, and where thieves break in and steal. But store up for yourselves treasures in heaven, where moth and rust do not destroy, and where thieves do not break in and steal. For where your treasure is, there your heart will be also.*
> Matthew 6:19-21

What do you long for more than anything else in the world?

_____

What's an example of how that "treasure" affects the things you say and do?

_____

Is it something with an eternal value? Or is it something that won't last?

_____

Put My Heart Where It Belongs

Now is a good time to pray about what's important to you—where your heart is. You could pray along these lines: "Jesus, I want you to be most important to me, but I know I'm putting a lot of value on lesser things like _____ . Those things are trying to steal my heart. I'm setting my heart on you now and making you my treasure. You're better than gold, praise, popularity, or anything else on earth. You are my Lord, and I want to live like it."

☐ DAY THREE

Deeper than Skin Deep

"**H**ave you seen that GORGEOUS new student at school?" We're so conscious of how people look! A great-looking new student or teacher sends gossip waves down the halls at school. Or a person who wears the latest hair style or clothes or make-up—we like anything that grabs the attention of our eyes.

Seeing Past the Surface

God created physical beauty and it's obvious he enjoys it—but he doesn't rank physical beauty number one in his priorities. He values internal character more. Yet how often does a deeply compassionate person, or a self-sacrificing person, or a humble person make waves in your school hallways? God once sent the prophet Samuel to anoint one of the sons of Jesse as the new king over Israel, only he didn't tell Samuel right away *which* son it would be. Here's what happened:

> *When they arrived, Samuel saw Eliab and thought, "Surely the Lord's anointed stands here before the Lord."*
> *But the Lord said to Samuel, "Do not consider his appearance or his height, for I have rejected him. The Lord does not look at the things man looks at. Man looks at the outward*

appearance, but the Lord looks at the heart." 1 Samuel 16:6-7

You can read the rest of the account in verses 8-13: David, the brother everybody thought was the least, turned out to be God's choice.

What You and I Can't See

When I'm getting along okay in life, going through the right actions of church and clubs and community, I catch myself congratulating myself for how well I'm doing. God's question is not, "How good do you look?" but, "Where's your heart?"

How about you? Are you voted Best Super Citizen of the School—and secretly gloat because you swung a few deciding votes by telling an embarrassing old story about the runner-up? (And it wasn't even a lie!)

Do your straight A's in science make you feel superior to the jocks who can't do anything but throw a football? Or vice versa—do you look down at the intellectuals as you collect the sports trophies?

God sees what people can't. He sees the heart.

Heart-Cleaning

God specializes in cleansing the heart which gets sick of phoniness and false appearances. If you're like Eliab—good on the outside, lacking on the inside—have the courage to examine your real motives. Then with confidence ask the Lord to cleanse you, because Jesus died for every single wrong thing you find in your heart. You might pray like this:

"Thank you, Lord, for showing me who I really am. Thank you for sticking with me and loving me even though I don't deserve it. Forgive me for each hidden sin I'm confessing to you now. Thank you, Lord, for your forgiveness that reaches deep down inside me."

☐ DAY FOUR

Who Can I Trust?

"**A**liens infiltrate the UN! Eyewitnesses say UFOs use UN building as teleport!"

Personally, I don't trust the headlines in those know-it-all newspapers by the check-out lanes in the grocery store. Why not? Because their "facts" (usually sensational rumors) seldom prove to be reliable. If you believed everything you read in those papers, you'd be paranoid—or at least confused.

The One Worthy of Trust

Some people are very trusting; they believe everything they read and hear, and they get into trouble for it. Other people, especially if they've been hurt by someone they relied on, hang back from trusting anybody.

Who and what we *trust* makes a difference in how we *think* and *act*. Jesus, who was in a position to know, said that the Lord is the only one who can be fully trusted with every part of our lives.

When we choose to trust the Lord (and trust is first of all a decision, not a feeling) it's going to make a difference in the way we live every day.

For example, if we trust God, we'll worry less about outward things because they're not so important. We won't be as frustrated by our own weaknesses and failings because we have his strength to rely on. Trusting him will change our behavior and our feelings—radically.

Who Can I Depend On?

As you read Matthew 6:25-34, you'll be reminded of several areas of life where you can choose to trust God (or to trust yourself or something else). Compare what Jesus said with how you normally go through life, and make it into a prayer. For example, he said:

> *And why do you worry about clothes? See how the lilies of the field grow. They do not labor or spin. Yet I tell you that not even Solomon in all his splendor was dressed like one of these. If that is how God clothes the grass of the field, which is here today and tomorrow is thrown into the fire, will he not much more clothe you, O you of little faith?* Matthew 6:28-30

After reading that, you could pray: "Lord, I'm very conscious of wearing the right thing, and I've been spending too much money on clothes. When I can't afford the latest, I feel self-conscious. I'm deciding now to trust you instead—what you provide for me to wear is okay, in style or not, because you look at my heart and not my outward show." Get the idea? Re-read the Scripture and write down a prayer:

_____

_____

_____

W·E·E·K T·H·R·E·E

☐ DAY FIVE

Heart Makeover

When was the last "failure" day you had? You know—when you tried extra-hard to choose the right things and failed anyway? You gritted your teeth trying to be nice and wound up with a tension headache. Or else you forgot about choosing God's way until you suddenly remembered him when the day was all over.

Failure can be good for us! Yes, that's right! For one thing, failure shows us we aren't able (in our own strength) to live up to God's laws.

Written on the Inside

Now *if* the Lord's commands are nothing but a list of demands posted on a wall, we'll give ourselves ulcers trying to live up to them, and we'll flop anyhow. Or else we'll give up and say, "Why try? It's easier to sin!"

But God promises to write his laws on another wall—the inner wall of our hearts—so his will becomes part of us.

> "The time is coming," declares the Lord, "when I will make a new covenant with the house of Israel and the house of Judah . . . I will put my law in their minds and write it on their hearts. I will be their God, and they will be my people

> *... they will all know me, from the least of them to the greatest,"* declares the Lord. *"For I will forgive their wickedness and will remember their sins no more."* Jeremiah 31:31-34

Read the entire passage (verses 31-34) to get the drift of what God promised to do. God's promise of a "new covenant" was fulfilled in Christ, as Hebrews 8 and 10 explain.

Newness—Inside!

When we accept Christ, all our striving to please God is replaced by a new relationship with him. He internalizes his laws so they begin to become part of us. It's a process, and God is a lot more patient about it than we are.

Are there ways you feel like you're trying too hard? Give it to God now in prayer. You might pray like this:

"Lord, you're the only one who can make my heart new. I try to be a 'good Christian' and I fail. Here's where I've been falling down: _____.
Thanks for your patience with me and how you pick me up every time I fail. With your help, today can be better. Live through me today, Lord, and help me remember you're always with me."

☐ Week · Four

Forks in the Road

W·E·E·K F·O·U·R

☐ **DAY ONE**

Easy to Say, Hard to Do

How do you tell if somebody is a Christian? Is it if the person . . .
    wears cross-shaped jewelry?
    goes to church every Sunday?
    carries a Bible to school?
    doesn't swear?

Those are all fine things, and we tend to "peg" a person as a Christian if he or she does them. But how do they measure up in a real test of the heart?

Here's how Jesus said his disciples could be identified:

> *A new command I give you: Love one another. As I have loved you, so you must love one another. By this all men will know that you are my disciples, if you love one another.* John 13:34-35

A Choice, Not a Feeling

Oh . . . you mean Jesus said the way people will know I'm a Christian is if I love other Christians?

Yes.

But that's not easy!

No. Especially when those other Christians include the most

stuck-up person in your youth group—or a pastor who has fallen into sin and disappointed an entire congregation—or a youth choir member who sneers at you when you hit a wrong note.

We can choose to love those people anyway, not waiting for a mushy feeling to come along and hit us, but making up our minds to seek their good instead of their harm.

Choose or Lose

No matter how easy-going we are, there's always *somebody* we have a hard time loving and caring about. God seems to put those people in our lives so we constantly have to decide whether to follow his way or not. Choose to love them, regardless of how you feel, and you'll find his love growing in you. You'll soon surprise yourself with the resources of love you find within yourself—from God.

It's much easier to wear a cross necklace and carry a Bible than it is to love another faulty human being. But love is also much closer to God's heart than jewelry or what we carry to school.

If you can keep this book away from prying eyes, write down the names of people you find hard to love:

_____

_____

Now pray specifically for each person whose name you wrote and for yourself in relation to that person. Like this: "Lord, help _____ with some special need today. When I have to see and talk to _____ , keep my heart open to be more understanding. Show me how I can even do _____ a favor today. I'm relying on you to love this person in and through me. And thank you for loving me—I'm not so easy to love either."

W·E·E·K F·O·U·R

☐ DAY TWO

Jesus' Top Two

A low rumble of conversation rises from the little group of people. Now and then a voice rises in angry argument. Jesus, in the middle of the circle, is calm. Some self-righteous people are questioning him—not out of a desire to learn God's ways, but in an attempt to trip him up with trick questions about Jewish law.

One religious teacher has his heart in the right place. He's so impressed with how Jesus' answers get to the heart of the matter that he asks his own straightforward question: "Of all the commandments, which is the most important?" Jesus uses Scripture to give his question a two-part answer:

> "The most important one," answered Jesus, "is this: 'Hear, O Israel, the Lord our God, the Lord is one. Love the Lord your God with all your heart and with all your soul and with all your mind and with all your strength.' The second is this: 'Love your neighbor as yourself.' There is no commandment greater than these." Mark 12:28-31

Two-Way Love

In other words God wants everything we do to come from the motive of love. So should we wait for ooey-gooey feelings before we do anybody a favor? Some people will be in for a long wait in that case!

God's love doesn't mean feelings; it means caring for another person and desiring the best for that person *regardless* of how we feel about him. Love like that takes courage and strength of will.

When the teacher seemed to be asking for one great commandment, Jesus gave him two. Loving *people* follows so naturally from loving God that the two can't be separated. Some people call the two loves "vertical" (up toward God) and "horizontal" (out toward other people). No matter what image helps you visualize the command, it's the same message: If we want to make our decisions in life according to God's will, they will be decisions based on love.

Living and Loving: How Do I Measure Up?

Are there some ways you've been separating your love from God from your love for people? Now is a good time to talk with God and ask him to put your heart together in those two areas. (For example, if you've been faithfully going to church to show your love for Jesus, but ignoring a particular person at church because he's boring.) Make a few prayer notes here.

_____

_____

If you feel a lack in the first commandment, loving God, pray about that too. Be brave enough to tell God that you haven't been putting him first, and ask him to rearrange your values.

Thank him for being a God who puts love first. What better thing could he ask you to build your life on?

☐ DAY THREE

Fatal Envy

When you envy somebody, how do you show it?
　　I tend to ignore/avoid the person (so I don't have to deal with seeing what he's got that I haven't got, and so I don't have to acknowledge my feelings). Or sometimes I'm super-nice to the person (to his face) to try to hide and deny my feelings.
　　There are lots of ways envy comes out. Early on in the history of the human race, it showed itself in murder.

A Negative Example

Jesus sets the example for everything positive in the Bible, but there are also plenty of examples of the negative. Writing about love, John chose Cain as an example of the opposite of love:

> *This is the message you heard from the beginning: We should love one another. Do not be like Cain, who belonged to the evil one and murdered his brother. And why did he murder him? Because his own actions were evil and his brother's were righteous.* 1 John 3:11-12

A Feeling... a Choice

Nice guy, that Cain. It would be dangerous to be too nice around him—he might kill you. You can read the full story of Cain's revenge in Genesis 4.

Cain naturally felt inner turmoil when he saw Abel leading a better life than his. How did he *choose to respond* to those feelings? He could have gone to work on his own life to become more godly; instead, he got rid of the competition. The killing wasn't even in a "fit of rage;" Genesis 4:8 makes it clear that it was a carefully planned attack.

Envy Kills

One way or the other, envy is a killer. It eats away at us inside. It leads us to kill the person we envy—if not physically, then in our hearts. The greatest passage on love in the Bible makes the specific point "Love . . . does not envy" (1 Corinthians 13:4).

Then how do we deal with envy, besides killing off the competition? We bring it to God. Envy says we're unhappy with how God has dealt things out. Surrendering to God's will is the best beginning for a cure for envy.

If there's any way you're feeling jealous, bring it to the Lord in prayer now. As much as you can, accept what he has given you. Ask him to help you decide to treat that other (envied) person in a way that comes from love.

Then watch for a change in your attitude toward the person you've been envying. You'll probably even see needs that person has—needs you can help with. And you'll find joy in helping the person you used to grind your teeth over.

W·E·E·K F·O·U·R

☐ DAY FOUR

Love in Action

"I'll call you sometime."
"Let's go out for pizza one of these days."
"We'll have to get together soon."

It's easy to say good words, even to have good intentions—then never get around to following through. Often I have warm thoughts about helping somebody out—a lot more often than I actually get around to picking up that phone or writing that letter.

Put Love into Action

Good thing for us Christ didn't stay in heaven, thinking nice thoughts about how he'd like to save mankind—someday. He *did* it. He arrived on earth and went through with God's plan, unpleasant as it was. That's God's love in action.

> *This is how we know what love is: Jesus Christ laid down his life for us. And we ought to lay down our lives for our brothers. If anyone has material possessions and sees his brother in need but has no pity on him, how can the love of God be in him? Dear children, let us not love with words or tongue but with actions and in truth.* 1 John 3:16-18

God Did Something...

Now is a good time to stop and thank the Lord for putting his love into action. We wouldn't be Christians at all if he hadn't done that.

When we know God acts on *his* love, it's easier to find the courage to put *our* love into action. God isn't asking us to do something he hasn't done first. Christ has been down this road of self-giving ahead of us.

...So Will I

What are some good intentions you've had—that you haven't gotten around to doing anything about?

What are some opportunities to show people you love them—that you haven't taken yet?

Thank God for putting his love into action, and pray for his strength to put the love he's given you into action. Go on—get specific about one love-filled thing to do today. Write your idea here:

_____

As you put your love into action today, keep thinking of Christ's example and thanking him that in this dangerous journey of giving yourself, he went first!

W·E·E·K F·O·U·R

☐ DAY FIVE

The Source of My Choices

Here's something that should be read several times, and slowly. You'll discover the source of love and the logical result of that love.

> Dear friends, let us love one another, for love comes from God. Everyone who loves has been born of God and knows God. Whoever does not love does not know God, because God is love. This is how God showed his love among us: He sent his one and only Son into the world that we might live through him. This is love: not that we loved God, but that he loved us and sent his Son as an atoning sacrifice for our sins. Dear friends, since God so loved us, we also ought to love one another. No one has ever seen God; but if we love each other, God lives in us and his love is made complete in us. 1 John 4:7-12

As you quietly take time to look at your own life, write down some thoughts and reactions to what you've just read:

_____

_____

_____

Sources and Results

According to this Scripture, there's one source of love. It isn't the generosity of my heart or my overflowing belief in the goodness of humanity. Humanity does some pretty awful things, and my own heart's goodness isn't so great either. There's only one source of real love: God.

There's one great evidence of God's love: it isn't the world he made or the happiness he gives us, but the fact that he gave his Son for us.

And there's one logical result of God's love for us: we love each other. Unselfishly and whether anybody deserves it or not—with God's help we love each other.

Go Back to the Source

As you meditated on today's Scripture, did you find yourself thanking God for loving you? Thanks comes naturally when we realize how much God loves us!

Did you find yourself not quite fulfilling the measure of loving others? Confess that honestly to the Lord, who is the source of love.

Ask for his love in you as a gift—straight from the Source. You can count on him to work on your heart and your will, so you find yourself caring about people you never cared about before.

I Can't Do It Alone

Pray about the thoughts you wrote earlier. (Maybe they *were* prayers.) Here's how one person prayed after reading this Scripture: "Lord, thank you for showing me what love looks like and acts like in Christ. You *are* love, and I can't love anybody unless you help me. I've tried to be loving on my own, but I fail. Live your love in me the rest of this day, Lord."

☐ Week・Five

What's Easy and What's Right

W·E·E·K F·I·V·E

☐ DAY ONE

Something to Stand On

"Lord, should I forgive that person who lied about me and got me kicked off the yearbook staff?"

"God, should I sneak around and go to that place my parents told me not to? I can get my friend to cover for me."

"Lord, should I tell my teacher that you came to die for him? He says he's an atheist."

Bring any of these questions—and a thousand others—to God, through praying and reading his Word. You'll never get this from him: "Uh . . . well . . . uh . . . golly, I'm not sure, why don't you ask somebody else?" God may not always give you the answer you'd *like* or an easy answer; but he'll always give you his honest answer about what you should decide to do. Remember a specific time when God answered your prayer—whether you *liked* his answer or not!

He Communicates!

The Lord has told us so much about what he wants for us. Sure there are issues the Bible isn't crystal-clear about. There are a lot more issues it *is* clear about, and we can confidently go to the Word for guidance.

Think of an area in which you need God's guidance. Have you dug into God's book for his help?

> *The law of the Lord is perfect,*
>   *reviving the soul.*
> *The statutes of the Lord are trustworthy,*
>   *making wise the simple.*
> *The precepts of the Lord are right,*
>   *giving joy to the heart.*
> *The commands of the Lord are radiant,*
>   *giving light to the eyes.*
> *The fear of the Lord is pure,*
>   *enduring forever.*
> *The ordinances of the Lord are sure*
>   *and altogether righteous.*
> *They are more precious than gold,*
>   *than much pure gold;*
> *they are sweeter than honey,*
>   *than honey from the comb.*
> *By them is your servant warned;*
>   *in keeping them there is great reward.* Psalm 19:7-11

You Can Trust the Bible

Yes, you *can* still trust the Bible in an age that says it's out-dated. It's trustworthy because God is still trustworthy.

Other standards shout at us from all sides. The standard of It Feels Good; the standard of It'll Make You Rich; the standard of Everybody's Doing It. They all want you to judge your actions by their on-again-off-again come-and-go morality. What "everybody's" doing today isn't what "everybody" will be doing tomorrow; what "felt good" yesterday might give you a lethal disease today.

The Lord's ways are eternal. You can still safely base your decisions, big and "small," on what his Word tells you.

Thank God now for his trustworthiness. He's sticking with you in good times and bad times, guiding you in times of doubt as well as times of faith.

And praise him for giving you his Word. He could have given you a little four-page pamphlet, but he gave you a volume you can study all your life and never come to the end of its beauty and wisdom.

WEEK FIVE

☐ DAY TWO

Okay for Me, Tough for You

How does it feel to be treated unfairly? You're bound to have an answer for that, because everybody gets the short end of the deal some time—some people more often than others.

Unfairness happens when I decide to ignore God's ways and treat other people on the basis of convenience—what's easiest for me, not what's best for you. Like this: I'll loan you my history notes because you'll be nice to me in return and let me use your motorcycle. However, if that motorcycle breaks down, I'm taking my history notes back. As for my friend who doesn't have something to offer me, well, there's no way he's getting anything out of me!

Unequal Forgiveness

Jesus told a parable about a person who was very generously forgiven, and who then decided it wasn't convenient to show forgiveness to another person. You can read it (and the question that gave rise to it) in Matthew 18:21-35. Here's part of the story:

> *Therefore, the kingdom of heaven is like a king who wanted to settle accounts with his servants . . . A man who owed him ten thousand talents was brought to him . . . The*

servant fell on his knees before him. "Be patient with me," he begged, "and I will pay back everything." The servant's master took pity on him, canceled the debt and let him go. But when that servant went out, he found one of his fellow servants who owed him a hundred denarii. He grabbed him and began to choke him. "Pay back what you owe me!" he demanded.
Matthew 18:23-24, 26-28

What's Good May Not Be What's Easy

It felt good for the servant when he was freed from that huge debt—just as it feels good for us when the Lord forgives us. But, when he saw the other fellow, he thought it would also feel good to be paid back those hundred denarii. A hundred denarii is astronomically smaller than ten thousand talents. The equally astronomical unfairness of his actions didn't even bother him.

Making our decisions on the basis of what's convenient for us is quick and easy. It's like eating a whole plate of brownies—gobble, gobble, yum. We don't even have to think about it. But it's just as sure to make us sick as deciding things by convenience will make us sick spiritually.

Have you ever made a choice at someone else's expense just because it was easier for you? Describe what happened.

_____

_____

Help Me Slow Down and Think

Easy isn't always right. Jesus didn't do the easy thing (which would have been to avoid this earth or, if he came here, to live a pampered and comfortable life). He did what was hard—and what was right.

Today you can count on the Lord to help you slow down and think about your choices. When you're tempted to do what's quickest, easiest, and most convenient, he'll be there to remind you that it might not be the best.

As you pray about decisions you'll be making today, ask for eyes to look past the comforts of the quick and easy.

W·E·E·K F·I·V·E

☐ DAY THREE

Hold on . . . He's Holding onto You

Teach me, O Lord, the way of thy statutes;
  and I will keep it to the end.
Give me understanding, that I may keep thy law
  and observe it with my whole heart.
Lead me in the path of thy commandments,
  for I delight in it.
Incline my heart to thy testimonies,
  and not to gain!
Turn my eyes from looking at vanities;
  and give me life in thy ways.
Confirm to thy servant thy promise,
  which is for those who fear thee.
Turn away the reproach which I dread;
  for thy ordinances are good.
Behold, I long for thy precepts;
  in thy righteousness give me life! Psalm 119:33-40, RSV

In every line of this part of Psalm 119—for that matter, in nearly every line of the entire long psalm—the writer makes an earnest wish and prayer that God will keep him on the right path. It's as though he knows a constant struggle in his heart to keep close to God.

When I wake up to the fact that I've been doing something

self-centered (again) I wonder: won't choosing God's ways ever become automatic? Why won't his laws ever be the easiest choice for me?

A War without End?

So does this battle go on forever?

As long as my inborn sin nature is in me—and it will be there till I die—I'll tend to be pulled away from obeying the Lord. So I'll always have to consciously stick to him and hold onto his ways.

The struggle to obey can get very discouraging! Then this psalm reminds me that all the "holding on" doesn't have to be done by me! The Lord is already holding onto me tighter than I'm holding onto him.

Trusting His Love

Notice this psalm writer didn't make all kinds of noble promises that he would stay faithful to God; he relied on God to stay faithful to him. He asked the Lord to teach *him,* lead *him,* turn *his* heart around.

Are you struggling with your choices? Do you find yourself constantly doing what's quickest and easiest, not thinking of the Lord till much later? List your top three struggles here:

_____

_____

_____

Never despair in your process of learning to make choices for God. He's in there with you. He's in your heart, working on you and helping you fight against sin. He'll forgive when you fail.

Spend time now telling the Lord you're glad he's holding onto you. Pray about the struggles you listed today. Trust his love for you, and let that love take over your life and your choices. Ask for his forgiveness where you need it. And look forward to a good day with him, secure in his acceptance.

W·E·E·K F·I·V·E

☐ DAY FOUR

When Trouble Knocks, Don't Answer

Do you ever get tempted by people who'd like you to join them in their sin?

Why don't they leave you alone? Maybe misery loves company. Maybe they want to use you to help them succeed in their schemes. You can be sure of one thing: they don't have what's best for you in mind.

Yet at that moment of temptation, sin looks very attractive and fun. A promise of money, pleasure, power—even getting out of studying—looks good in the short run.

But the Lord says, "Wait a minute! Are you more interested in what's easy or what's right?"

(Struggle, struggle . . .) "Okay, Lord, I want what's right. Even though it seems it would be nice to have that stolen tape or those stolen test answers, it'd be wrong and I'd be miserable."

Stand Up to 'em

Maybe people can't tempt you to steal because stealing doesn't tempt you. What does? How you talk? How you act on dates? Where you go after school (or even during school)?

Read Proverbs 1:10-19 and you'll get a description of other people tempting you to sin that (we hope) is worse than anything you've run into, no matter how bad your high school is! A sample:

> *"Come along with us; let's lie in wait for someone's blood, let's waylay some harmless soul; let's swallow them alive, like the grave, and whole, like those who go down to the pit; we will get all sorts of valuable things and fill our houses with plunder."* Proverbs 1:11-13

Even if you've never been tempted to rob or kill somebody, have you been tempted to go along when other people "assassinate" somebody's character? Or when they "rob" somebody of his reputation?

> *"If sinners entice you, do not give in to them . . . do not go along with them, do not set foot on their paths . . . These men lie in wait for their own blood; they waylay only themselves!"* Proverbs 1:10, 15, 18

Decide Ahead of Time

The pull of the crowd, even the pull of one influential friend, is tough to resist. It's especially tough when we're making up our minds right on the spur of the moment.

The time to decide Christ's way is ahead of time, when we're calm, before the temptation arrives. Stealing is out . . . sex is for marriage . . . ripping up other people verbally is off limits . . . I'll earn my money honestly or not at all . . . and so on. Then our minds are already made up, *before* the storm of temptation hits.

Anticipate some of the temptations you will face today and this week.

_____

_____

Prayer-full Decisions

Now, in front of the Lord, make up your mind about some particular temptation you *know* is going to hit you today. Decide now you'll do what he wants in that situation, so when it happens you won't have to make a two-second decision based on how you feel right then. Ask to feel his presence right when the temptation hits. And thank him for getting you through it!

W·E·E·K F·I·V·E

☐ DAY FIVE

Now and Forever

Sometimes it seems like nothing in life *lasts*. You have a best friend and she moves away; you've taken all the classes your favorite teacher offers; football season ends; your arms get too long for your favorite leather jacket; graduation rushes at you before you're ready.

Of course there *is* something permanent. It's God himself. And since you're basing your life decisions on him, isn't it good to know he'll stay around and not change his mind about what he wants for you?

Our God Is Forever

Here's part of what Psalm 119 has to say about God's permanence:

> *Your word, O Lord, is eternal;*
>   *it stands firm in the heavens.*
> *Your faithfulness continues through all generations;*
>   *you established the earth, and it endures.*
> *Your laws endure to this day,*
>   *for all things serve you.* Psalm 119:89-91

Why is it good to know that God is eternal and his Word doesn't change? Write down some of your thoughts about that:

_____

_____

_____

Somebody to Depend On

Now you can turn your thoughts into praise! Re-read the portion of Psalm 119 again and for each line make up your own praise (applause, honor, congratulations) to the Lord for being somebody you can depend on.

v.89 _____

_____

v.90 _____

_____

v.91 _____

_____

If you like, try to make up a song about the Lord's eternal-ness. You can use a melody you dream up, or a borrowed melody. Use this space for your song:

Sing it to him—he'll enjoy it even if your voice isn't star quality!

☐ *Week · Six*

My Choices and My Friends

W·E·E·K S·I·X

☐ DAY ONE

Bickering Is for Babies

Tom was a great youth minister! The high schoolers at his church had all the best in Sunday school, Bible Study, service opportunities, camp-outs, and other fun activities. While he was at the church, the youth group doubled in size. But eventually Tom left the church for another job, and the youth group dwindled to just a few.

So what was the problem? It certainly wasn't Tom's fault, but some of the young people in his group had become devoted to him instead of devoted to the Lord first. When he left, they moved on to find another dynamic leader somewhere else.

Acting Like Children

Do Christians really split into different camps over their favorite leaders? You bet they do. Teens do it; adults do it. In Paul's day they were holding a popularity contest between Paul and Apollos. Paul wrote to the Corinthians about the issue—not to get them on his side, but to tell them they were acting like children in their jealousy and quarreling.

> *Brothers, I could not address you as spiritual but as worldly—mere infants in Christ. I gave you milk, not solid food, for you were not yet ready for it. Indeed, you are still not*

ready. You are still worldly. For since there is jealousy and quarreling among you, are you not worldly? Are you not acting like mere men? For when one says, "I follow Paul," and another, "I follow Apollos," are you not mere men? What, after all, is Apollos? And what is Paul? Only servants, through whom you came to believe—as the Lord has assigned to each his task. 1 Corinthians 3:1-5

Say Goodbye to Childish Christianity

Paul is chastising the Corinthians for being like babies—too young for real food, having to be spoon-fed. Christian leaders like pastors and youth leaders can teach, inspire, and enlighten us. But each of us has to follow Christ himself and make his own decisions based on the Word. There's bound to be less quarreling when we're all following Jesus than when we're following our modern "Pauls" and Apolloses."

So Where Do You Stand?

Do you ever find yourself taking the word of teachers and other leaders without checking it out in Scripture and prayer to determine for yourself what God is all about? Think of a time when this happened to you.

_____

_____

Have you ever heard of a situation where Christians bickered over their leaders (this is rather common, unfortunately)?

_____

_____

Follow Jesus

Ask the Lord to help you see more and more clearly what God wants you to do and be. Ask him to help you discern his truth when opinions and quarrels confuse the issues.

W·E·E·K S·I·X

☐ DAY TWO

Attitude Check

Say the Lord told you to give $10 a week to support your church. You're obeying, but in order to do it, you had to stop going to movies—a good exercise in self-discipline for you, because you were spending too much time and money on the movies.

Now you're (secretly) kind of proud of yourself. You want everybody else to be as spiritual as you are. Maybe you've even turned into an anti-movie crusader.

You cruise past the local cinema to see who from church is going in, and you add up how much they could and should be giving to the church instead. In your youth group and Sunday school you request studies on topics like "Wasting God's Money" and "Compromising with the World." If anybody tries to defend movie-going, they find themselves in a fierce debate with you.

The Real Question

So who's right about the movie issue?

Would you be surprised to know that when the Bible talks about issues like this—where Christians disagree on what's right and wrong—the Bible usually doesn't settle the issue, but focuses instead on attitudes and acceptance? Here's an example:

> *Accept him whose faith is weak, without passing judgment on disputable matters. One man's faith allows him to eat everything, but another man, whose faith is weak, eats only vegetables. The man who eats everything must not look down on him who does not, and the man who does not eat everything must not condemn the man who does, for God has accepted him. Who are you to judge someone else's servant? To his own master he stands or falls. And he will stand, for the Lord is able to make him stand.* Romans 14:1-4

When you're trying to make decisions based on God's will, you start feeling good about what you're deciding and how you're living. In fact you can feel so good about it that you want everybody else to decide the same way you do. And a peculiar temptation rises: the urge to make everybody else come to the same conclusions about things that you have.

In other words you could be technically right in your movies/money decision but overwhelmingly wrong in your self-righteousness.

Accept Anyway

As you look at Christians around you and look at your own heart, bring your attitudes to the Lord. Do you feel superior to anybody because you think you're acting better than he or she is? Think of

a recent time when you felt "better." _____
Pray for yourself, that you'll show Christ's acceptance to people who don't do things your way.

And pray for those Christians whose behavior irks you because it isn't quite the way you would do things. Don't pray they'll see the light and be like you; pray that God will lead them, even if he leads them on a path slightly different from yours.

WEEK SIX

☐ DAY THREE

Different Worship for Different People

A certain church met at 4:00 Sunday afternoon because they were renting the facilities of another church and 4:00 was when the building was free. One friend of mine heard about the unusual worship time and was shocked. "That's a strange time for a church to meet!" she said.

Well, is 10:30 Sunday morning sacred? Of course not—not according to the Bible. Yet how easy it is to look down on Christians who have chosen to honor God a little differently from the way we do it.

What's Inside?

Does your pastor wear a robe? How about your choir? Is the choir in the back or the front of the church? Do you go forward for communion? Do you ever sing contemporary songs or only traditional hymns? Do you raise your hands in worship?

Many Christians argue about whether to do those things and a hundred others. Meanwhile God is asking, "*Why* are you doing those things?"

You can raise your hands to sincerely praise the Lord, or you can raise your hands because everybody else is doing it. The same is true for every other aspect of worship. Here's how Paul wrote about differing opinions:

One man considers one day more sacred than another; another man considers every day alike. Each one should be fully convinced in his own mind. He who regards one day as special, does so to the Lord. He who eats meat, eats to the Lord, for he gives thanks to God; and he who abstains, does so to the Lord and gives thanks to God. For none of us lives to himself alone and none of us dies to himself alone. If we live, we live to the Lord; and if we die, we die to the Lord. So, whether we live or die, we belong to the Lord. Romans 14:5-7

Pray for Other Churches

When Christians disagree, it can either be ugly or it can be a demonstration of love. If we disagree in a condemning way, outsiders look at us and don't see any difference between us Christians and them. But if we "agree to disagree" and still love each other, the world will be impressed.

Today, pray for other churches. Pray specifically for young people you know who worship and follow Christ in different ways than you do. Pray for their pastors and other leaders. Pray for the ones whose style bothers you the most. Make a prayer list here.

_____

_____

_____

Your heart will warm up as you wish God's best for these fellow-believers. Make plans to learn more about them and why they worship as they do. You might gain some new brothers and sisters in the Lord as well as widening your own heart!

WEEK SIX

☐ DAY FOUR

Yeah, but He's Wrong!

I could just *see* what my friend was doing to himself—the sin he was falling into, and the mess he was making of his life. "Acceptance" didn't promise much hope for him, because he needed to *change*. Or was I being too judgmental?

You're Right; They're Wrong

When the Lord tells us to accept each other as we are, he doesn't mean to be blind and stupid about other people's sins. Of course there will be times we can see that somebody else is wrong—dead wrong—in the decisions and choices he or she is making.

What do we do then? Stand back and smile in the name of "acceptance"? No—but neither should we condemn the person. We violently disagree with what the person is *doing*, but we still love the person. Galatians puts it this way:

> *Brothers, if someone is caught in a sin, you who are spiritual should restore him gently. But watch yourself, or you also may be tempted. Carry each other's burdens, and in this way you will fulfill the law of Christ.* Galatians 6:1-2

Bring Them Back, Lord

Today, think especially of people you know who are going the wrong way. Maybe they're destroying their relationships . . . they're ignoring God . . . they're all caught up in themselves . . . they're slaves to drugs or alcohol . . . they're scared of things they don't need to be afraid of . . . they think they're nothing when God says they're Something.

Pray for several people, bringing one specific problem of each one to the Lord. If you don't know exactly what to pray for, simply ask for God to do his will in that person. This list may help you pray:

"Lord, I pray for _____ that you will _____ _____."

"I pray that you'll help _____ to see that _____ _____."

"Please be with _____ and help this person to get over _____."

Write your own prayers for other people you care about who are going the wrong way:

_____
_____
_____

Don't Forget Me!

As you've prayed, you may have wanted to insert your own name in one of those blanks. Seeing other people's needs reminds us of how needy we are, too. Today's Scripture says that when we want to help someone who's sinning, we're likely to be tempted too—to join in the sin, perhaps, or to think we're "better."

So pray for yourself too, like this: "Lord, help my attitude toward _____ and help me to show your love to

_____ . Keep me from being drawn into

_____'s sin and from feeling superior to

_____ . And if you want, show me how to help

carry _____'s burden as your Word says."

W·E·E·K S·I·X

☐ DAY FIVE

For My Friend's Sake

A guy we know was, in his pre-Christian days, very heavily into hard rock music complete with the accompanying Satanism, drugs, and free sex—not to mention spending all his money buying albums. He feels that rock ruined his life. Now that he has Christ, he's become a passionate opponent of rock music of all types, including contemporary Christian rock.

Now I personally feel he goes overboard when he equates contemporary Christian musicians with Satan-obsessed groups who look like they just crawled out of the grave. Still, I would never invite him to go to a Christian concert with us (even by the most Spirit-filled singer) if it was going to have a rock sound.

Why not? Because for our friend who believes so passionately that it's wrong, going there would be a sin. *For him.* Attending the concert may not be wrong for anybody else in the audience, but it would be for him, because he would be violating his conscience. And we'd be helping him do it.

Free to Say "No"

What one person is free to do in the Lord, another one may not be free to do. Paul talks about this in Romans:

> *Let us therefore make every effort to do what leads to peace and to mutual edification. Do not destroy the work of God for the sake of good. All food is clean, but it is wrong for a man to eat anything that causes someone else to stumble. It is better not to eat meat or drink wine or to do anything else that will cause your brother to fall.* Romans 14:19-21

A Vote against Gloating

Say I feel free to listen to certain music, go to certain places, and watch certain movies. What does my freedom do to other Christians who sincerely believe those practices are wrong? If they look up to me, they may feel excused to do those things—and they'll suffer the pangs of guilt—real guilt. My show-off freedom may be nothing but pride anyway as I gloat about my "enlightenment" and the other person's "narrowness." So I'd better refrain, not for my sake, but for theirs.

What? Curtail my freedom? For somebody else? Yes, that's what this Scripture says. "Do not destroy the work of God for the sake of . . ." a concert. Or a movie. Or any other thing that's less than the life of a friend.

As you pray about your decisions of where to go and what to watch and listen to, remember Christian friends who are teetering on the edge of sin and may be influenced by observing you. Think of two people and situations where this could happen.

_____

_____

Pray for the nerve to put them first by saying "No" to yourself.

☐ Week · Seven

The High Cost of Jesus' Choice

W·E·E·K S·E·V·E·N

☐ **DAY ONE**

He Gave Up Heaven

Who wants to give up stuff for God? It doesn't sound very attractive— especially when everybody around you is into getting and having.

Jesus only asks us to do what he has done first. When he came to earth for us, here's what he went through:

> Your attitude should be the same as that of Christ Jesus:
> Who, being in very nature God,
>   did not consider equality with God
>   something to be grasped,
> but made himself nothing,
>   taking the very nature of a servant,
>   being made in human likeness.
> And being found in appearance as a man,
>   he humbled himself
>   and became obedient to death—
>   even death on a cross! Philippians 2:5-8

Humility Hurts

Jesus took a series of steps "down" to be here with us. First he let go of hanging on to his rights as God. Then he became a human being—not a king in a palace but a servant in our world. Then he obeyed God to the point of dying—even dying the death of a criminal on a cross.

When we get to heaven and see what it's like, we'll finally have some idea of what Jesus gave up in order to come here to live and die for us.

Joy, Not Gloom

What's our response to knowing how much Jesus gave up for us? We could go around gloomy at the thought of all he went through. We could be filled with guilt that Christ had to suffer so much for us. And it's true that we're filled with a sense of how little of his love we deserve (zero).

But it's our completely undeserving condition that makes us the happiest about what Jesus gave up for us! He proved he loves us by what he did. We can look up, not down, because he was willing to come here for us!

Instead of sticking your head under your pillow for shame, let Christ hear your gratefulness for what he did for you—and what he's still doing for you. If writing your praises and prayers is a help to you, fill up this space with thanks to the Lord for giving up heaven for you:

W·E·E·K S·E·V·E·N

☐ DAY TWO

Just Say No— to Yourself!

Isn't it fun to say "Yes" to yourself? "Yes, Self, I'll be glad to buy you that stereo for your birthday!" "Sure, self, you definitely need a new wardrobe for school—you can't let everybody see you in the same stuff you wore last year!" "Of course, Self, you obviously need that second piece of cherry pie, and how about some ice cream to go with it?"

Nobody Likes a "No"

Who wants to get "No" for an answer? We even get irritated with God when we pray for something and he (wisely) says No.

So the idea of saying no to *ourselves* is revolutionary!

It's Jesus' idea (revolutionary like many of his other ideas). Here's what he said:

> *"If anyone would come after me, he must deny himself and take up his cross daily and follow me. For whoever wants to save his life will lose it, but whoever loses his life for me will save it. What good is it for a man to gain the whole world, and yet lose or forfeit his very self?"* Luke 9:23-25

Get Out the Eraser?

"Deny yourself" sounds at first like "erase yourself." But you can't deny that you exist. God made you. He loves you. He accepts you. So what does Jesus mean by this everyday "denying"?

Once we take a close, fearless look at our hearts, we see all kinds of self-centeredness; we have a deep drive to get our own way. Jesus calls us to say "No" to that.

He asks us to contradict the self-indulgent urge. He asks us to choose against our self-pampering will and decide for him and for others (those two closely-connected great commandments).

Practice Saying "No"

Instead of getting out the eraser, practice saying "No." Not only to drugs, as the popular campaign says, but to the inner voice of Self which is always whining for its own way.

Expect a struggle when you set out to say "No" to yourself and "Yes" to God. He's in there with you in the middle of that struggle. Jesus already took up the cross he asks you to take up—literally. He understands.

Before you set out on today's activities, pray for the trust in God that will help you say "No" to self-will. Think of three particular areas in which you need to learn to say No.

_____

_____

_____

Talk with God about each of these. If you aren't even aware where you need to say No, ask God to make it clear to you as you go through this day with him.

☐ DAY THREE

Finishing What You Start

In the woods on a hill near my home was a scattered pile of cement blocks known as "Finley's Folly." Somebody named Finley had started to build a house and had given up on the project.

We have a few half-finished projects around our house too. The antique sink that we put in still has a gap between it and the wall. All the window frames and sills in the kitchen are painted, except the least convenient one behind the stove. Compost should be spread on the garden. And the list goes on . . .

Are you haunted by an abandoned weight-lifting program? Do you have an unfinished model of the *Titanic* or a half-read copy of *Moby Dick* under your bed? Ever started a diet and given it up? Lots of us have problems finishing what we start.

Half-finished Christians

On the fringes of your church or youth group there may be some Christians who started out with Christ in a blaze of glory. But then something happened. The flash faded and they dropped out. Gradually you realized you weren't seeing them around church anymore, and now when they see you coming, they duck.

What happens to those "half-finished Christians"? Some of them run into persecution they didn't expect as the old crowd or even family members reject them. Some pray for things and give up on God when he doesn't deliver. Some get disillusioned when the good feelings fade.

Jesus told a parable about a person who gave up:

> *"Suppose one of you wants to build a tower. Will he not first sit down and estimate the cost to see if he has enough money to complete it? For if he lays the foundation and is not able to finish it, everyone who sees it will ridicule him, saying, 'This fellow began to build and was not able to finish.'"* Luke 14:28-30

Do an Estimate First

The lesson? Jesus was being realistic with us, saying, "If you're going to make a commitment to me, stop and think about what it will cost you—because it is going to cost you." Jesus doesn't deceive us about the risks of following him.

Before you make God all kinds of promises, let him stop you while you consider the repercussions. Are you going to side with an underdog at school?—then are you really willing to lose some of your friends who pick on him? Will you actually stick with your commitment not to date a certain person who tempts you too much?—then what are you going to do when that person calls you?

Do an estimate in the space provided for something you want to promise the Lord.

_____

_____

The Lord won't kid you about the cost of following him. And neither will he abandon you—he'll help you make specific plans for coping with the cost. Bring him any of your fears about "What if?" and make your decisions, under his Lordship, about what you will do as you follow him.

W·E·E·K S·E·V·E·N

☐ DAY FOUR

Last Place?

"And our Disciple of the Year Award goes to . . . may I have the envelope, please . . . Simon Peter! Yes, Simon Peter is Jesus' Disciple of the Year for A.D. 33. In his travels with Jesus, Peter has shown himself consistently able to push himself to the front of the crowd and be the one who talks first, loudest, and most often. Besides that, Peter has demonstrated his ability to totally eclipse his brother Andrew, who is rumored also to be one of the twelve disciples even though we hardly ever hear about him."

What?? A Disciple of the Year Award? For being loud and pushy? Are we kidding?

Yes, we are. Unfortunately, Christians often compete to be the greatest-looking and ignore the example of Jesus in the process.

Oops! He Heard Us

Jesus once caught his twelve disciples in an embarrassing argument. Here's how it went:

> They came to Capernaum. When he was in the house, he asked them, "What were you arguing about on the road?" But they kept quiet because on the way they had argued about who was the greatest. Sitting down, Jesus called the Twelve and

said, "If anyone wants to be first, he must be the very last, and the servant of all." Mark 9:33-35

That was not the news the disciples wanted to hear! Their argument probably hadn't been so blatant as, "I'm the greatest!" "No, I am!" More likely they were saying things like, "I was with Jesus before any of you!" "Well I saw his very first miracle!" "Well I was the one who asked him to teach us to pray!" And so on. Good Christian-sounding credits.

Others First, Me Last

Christ turned all that argument upside-down. He said it's not the people who *sound* like spiritual champions who are the real servants of God. The "greatest" in God's kingdom are the ones who are willing to be the least and make others the most.

Are there areas of "serving God" where you're tempted to put yourself forward at others' expense? If you play the piano well, are you willing to give somebody else a chance to play on Sunday nights even if they're not as good as you are? If you pray beautifully out loud, can you keep your mouth shut and let the more shy people stumble through their prayers?

Witnessing, singing, helping people with problems, and teaching Bible studies can all be done from the desire to look like the best. Christ asks us to make others look good instead, not denying our gifts, but being willing to serve somebody else and lift up somebody else in our place.

Think of two abilities or talents that you could use either to make yourself look good or to be a servant.

_____

_____

You can surrender those areas where you're tempted to flaunt your abilities in Christian service. Ask the Lord to take them over and use you as he wants, not as you want. The "service" will become true service and you'll be happier and freer doing it!

W·E·E·K S·E·V·E·N

☐ DAY FIVE

The Shepherd Pays

Well, it's easy enough for Jesus to ask us to give up everything for him and endure the cost. He's in heaven, right? Enjoying the praises of angels and being at the right hand of his Father. What does he know about giving up anything?

He knows *a lot* about giving up everything! He gave up more than we'll ever have to. The path we walk has his footprints on it ahead of us. When he described himself as the "Good Shepherd," he went on to say this:

> "I am the good shepherd. The good shepherd lays down his life for the sheep. The hired hand is not the shepherd who owns the sheep. So when he sees the wolf coming, he abandons the sheep and runs away. Then the wolf attacks the flock and scatters it. The man runs away because he is a hired hand and cares nothing for the sheep.
> I am the good shepherd; I know my sheep and my sheep know me—just as the Father knows me and I know the Father—and I lay down my life for the sheep." John 10:11-15

An Infinite Price Tag

"Cost" almost seems like too mild a word for what the Son of

God paid for us, his sheep. Were we really worth all that? He says yes.

Think of Jesus' life and death, and write down some ideas of what he paid . . .
- physically?
- emotionally?
- to give up heaven?
- to give up the immediate presence of his Father?
- to experience death?

Let each of your thoughts lead into a prayer expressing your thanks to him for doing this for you—and for considering you worth it!

☐ *Week · Eight*

Real-life Choices: What Would Jesus Choose?

W·E·E·K E·I·G·H·T

☐ DAY ONE

When Temptation Bugs You...

> During the days of Jesus' life on earth, he offered up prayers and petitions with loud cries and tears to the one who could save him from death, and he was heard because of his reverent submission. Although he was a son, he learned obedience from what he suffered and, once made perfect, he became the source of eternal salvation for all who obey him. Hebrews 5:7-9

It's surprising to read that Jesus had to *learn* obedience to God, but there it is, right in the Bible.

That's an encouragement to me. I also struggle with learning to submit to God. I also beg God to get me out from under things. I also get tired of fighting off sin that wants to drag me away from God.

Jesus Struggled with Decisions?

Yes, Jesus faced the hard realities of repeatedly having to decide to do God's will in the face of everything that said to do otherwise. We read about his three temptations by Satan in the wilderness, but he must have been tempted daily all during his ministry.

How might Jesus have been tempted? Satan would have tried to get him to abandon his mission, ignore people's needs, blow his opponents away, proclaim himself earthly king, be proud . . . well, you know Satan has an inexhaustible bag of tricks. Was Jesus faced with temptations of money, power, sex, glory? Of course he was. But he submitted to God's will instead of submitting to the temptations.

I'm Not Alone

So if you struggle with deciding for God—or should we say *when* you struggle with deciding for God—you're in good company. Jesus went through those struggles too. In his weak human flesh he fought through those temptations and stuck with the Father. With his help, so will you.

As you pray today, think of Jesus going through each of your old familiar temptations with you victoriously. Ride his victory through that temptation. Write out anything you want to say to him about those temptations, including your thanks to him for being with you and winning the fight for you:

_____

_____

_____

W·E·E·K E·I·G·H·T

☐ DAY TWO

Slammed Doors, Blocked Plans

A high school senior friend talked for weeks about his plans to visit the college where he wants to enroll next fall. You could imagine the date of the coming visit circled in fluorescent orange on his calendar. The weekend came and went. "How was the trip to the university, John?" "Oh, I couldn't go. The night before we were going to leave, our car broke down."

Plans That Don't Work Out

Broken dreams! Our biggest plans, cherished for weeks or even years, can collapse in the face of a leaky gas line.

What do we do then? Cry? Sometimes. But after we cry, we can look for God's alternate idea. That's what Paul and his companions did when their planned missionary efforts were blocked by God's intervention. (As you read this passage, it will be interesting and helpful to look on a Bible map. Try to find one that shows "Paul's second missionary journey" as this trip is usually known.)

> *Paul and his companions traveled throughout the region of Phrygia and Galatia, having been kept by the Holy Spirit from preaching the word in the province of Asia. When they came to the border of Mysia, they tried to enter Bithynia, but*

the Spirit of Jesus would not allow them to. So they passed by Mysia and went down to Troas. During the night Paul had a vision of a man of Macedonia standing and begging him, "Come over to Macedonia and help us." After Paul had seen the vision, we got ready at once to leave for Macedonia, concluding that God had called us to preach the gospel to them.
Acts 16:6-10

Plan B?

Could God himself have been preventing these missionaries from going where they wanted to go? That's what it says. Regardless of how good their intentions were for going to Asia or Bithynia, right then the Lord wanted them to cross the Aegean Sea and go to Macedonia instead.

And they didn't pout or complain about their broken plans; they got on the boat and went to Macedonia. Humanly speaking, Macedonia looked like "Plan B;" actually it was God's "Plan A." On that trip a church was started in Philippi, to whom Paul later wrote the letter of Philippians which has blessed millions of people—you've read some of it in this book.

Turning Broken Plans into Prayers

Got any cherished dreams that have turned to dust? Write them down here.

_____

_____

Take them back to God and ask him what he has in mind. Be fearless about looking for his alternatives to what you wanted. Pray about your disappointments and allow God to heal them with the peace of being in his will.

W·E·E·K E·I·G·H·T

☐ DAY THREE

Thanks or No Thanks?

"Thank you."

Those are two of the most beautiful words in our language, and undoubtedly in any other language too. We don't hear them often enough. When we thank a person, we're saying, "I needed what you did for me." It's a way of honoring the person to whom we're grateful.

Even God likes to hear us say "Thank you!" It's up to us to decide to say it to him, or to decide to go along on our way and forget about him. That's clear from this incident that happened to Jesus:

> Now on his way to Jerusalem, Jesus traveled along the border between Samaria and Galilee. As he was going into a village, ten men who had leprosy met him. They stood at a distance and called out in a loud voice, "Jesus, Master, have pity on us!"
>
> When he saw them, he said, "Go, show yourselves to the priests." And as they went, they were cleansed.
>
> One of them, when he saw he was healed, came back, praising God in a loud voice. He threw himself at Jesus' feet and thanked him—and he was a Samaritan.
>
> Jesus asked, "Were not all ten cleansed? Where are the other nine? Was no one found to return and give praise to God

except this foreigner?" Then he said to him, "Rise and go; your faith has made you well." Luke 17:11-19

Thank You, Loud and Clear

How often I complain loudly, but when something good happens I barely mutter my thanks. The tenth leper had been calling out for Jesus' help "in a loud voice," and when he was healed, he thanked God "in a loud voice" too!

Thanking God is a deliberate decision we make every day. Gratitude doesn't come automatically or even easily; we have to concentrate on it until it becomes more of a habit.

An Attitude of Gratitude

It's a habit that rewards us. A thankful heart gets us through the days much more happily than a grouchy, complaining spirit. And God deserves our thanks for all the good things he gives us and does for us—and simply for being himself!

What better way to pray today than to say "Thank you, Lord!" for as many things as you can? Think of what you're grateful to him for in these areas and any others:

salvation:

relationships:

material things:

anything else:

W·E·E·K E·I·G·H·T

☐ DAY FOUR

He Could Have Passed By

In the preceding section you read about a Samaritan leper, the only one out of ten who thanked God for his healing. Samaritans, part-Jewish residents of an area north of Jerusalem and south of Galilee, were not popular with the Jews.

Several times Jesus singled out Samaritans for particular honor. The most familiar example is his parable which put the phrase "good Samaritan" into common English language.

> "A man was going down from Jerusalem to Jericho, when he fell into the hands of robbers. They stripped him of his clothes, beat him and went away, leaving him half dead. A priest happened to be going down the same road, and when he saw the man, he passed by on the other side. So too, a Levite, when he came to the place and saw him, passed by on the other side. But a Samaritan, as he traveled, came where the man was; and when he saw him, he took pity on him. He went to him and bandaged his wounds, pouring on oil and wine. Then he put the man on his own donkey, took him to an inn and took care of him. The next day he took out two silver coins and gave them to the innkeeper. 'Look after him,' he said, 'and when I return, I will reimburse you for any extra expense you may have.'" Luke 10:30-35

What's Good about the Good Samaritan

Three people in this story made decisions—all of them very clear, and all of them with definite consequences for the poor fellow who was lying on the rocks next to the road. The priest "passed by on the other side," and the Levite "passed by on the other side" (verses 31-32). They saw him; they knew what they should do; and they crossed the street instead.

Ouch! Have you ever literally crossed the street to avoid somebody? I have. I told myself I suddenly remembered I had to go to *that* store over there, but actually I was slipping away from some awkward or unpleasant encounter.

Fortunately for the beaten-up traveler, a third person came along and made a very different decision. The Samaritan "took pity on him . . . went to him and bandaged his wounds . . . put the man on his own donkey, took him to an inn and took care of him" (verses 33-34). He also went to some expense to see that the man was cared for after he left.

Whoa!

It was a simple decision for the Samaritan—to stop the donkey and go see how he could help—and it was a life-and-death decision from the point of view of the victim. Did the Samaritan struggle over it? We don't know. We only know what he did, and he did the right thing.

Today you're going to meet a few victims: people life has robbed and left by the road. The "holy" people in the parable decided to pass on by. The "lowly" person stopped and helped—maybe risking being robbed himself. Can you think of people you know at school or work or church who have hurts like these? Write their names here.

_____

_____

_____

Pray now, in advance, for the "beat-up" people you'll meet today. Ask God to make you a good Samaritan for them. And expect to find yourself standing and looking, having to make a decision. With God's help, you'll make the right one!

W·E·E·K E·I·G·H·T

☐ DAY FIVE

Jesus Chose His Father's Way

We end this book on making Christ-centered choices with the all-time most difficult and most far-reaching choice anybody ever had to make. It has affected us, you, and millions of other people. Jesus made it, and to say, "It wasn't easy" is almost flippant.

Christ was in the garden of Gethsemane and he knew he was about to be arrested and crucified. His disciples were falling asleep instead of praying with him. All his humanness cried out to escape the coming torture.

Read the account and imagine yourself right there through a few of the most dramatic minutes in history:

> *Going a little farther, he fell with his face to the ground and prayed, "My Father, if it is possible, may this cup be taken from me. Yet not as I will, but as you will."*
>
> *Then he returned to his disciples and found them sleeping. "Could you men not keep watch with me for one hour?" he asked Peter. "Watch and pray so that you will not fall into temptation. The spirit is willing, but the body is weak."*
>
> *He went away a second time and prayed, "My Father, if it is not possible for this cup to be taken away unless I drink it, may your will be done."*
>
> *When he came back, he again found them sleeping, be-*

cause their eyes were heavy. So he left them and went away once more and prayed the third time, saying the same thing.

Then he returned to the disciples and said to them, "Are you still sleeping and resting? Look, the hour is near, and the Son of Man is betrayed into the hands of sinners. Rise, let us go! Here comes my betrayer!" Matthew 26:39-46

With Us in the Balance

Nobody else has ever had to make a decision quite like that one. Jesus did not owe mankind any favors. He was going to die for us only because he loved us and God wanted us back. On the cross he would have to feel God's rejection of sin, though he had never done anything wrong. Tough? Difficult? A struggle? All our words are inadequate to describe Jesus' choice in Gethsemane. Our souls were in the balance.

And he decided for God, though everyone else had left him. It took him three times, going back and wrestling with it. At the end we can hear the confident finality in his voice as he strides out to meet Judas.

He'll Help Me Choose

What does all this long-ago struggle say to me, right now, as I face today's choices?

It says struggling over choices isn't sin. It's normal to have difficulty deciding to do God's will.

It says Christ understands the inner fight to be godly. He has been there. It happened to him too.

It says God pulls for the person who wants to do his will even if he has a hard time doing it.

And it says victory is possible. With God's help, we can and will decide the right way, pleasant or unpleasant, popular or unpopular. We can do it.

Today, before you make another decision, decide to ask the Lord to guide every choice you make. Thank him for understanding the conflicts you experience as you choose for him. And above all, thank him for his promise to get you through the difficult times, as he got Jesus through, by his grace.